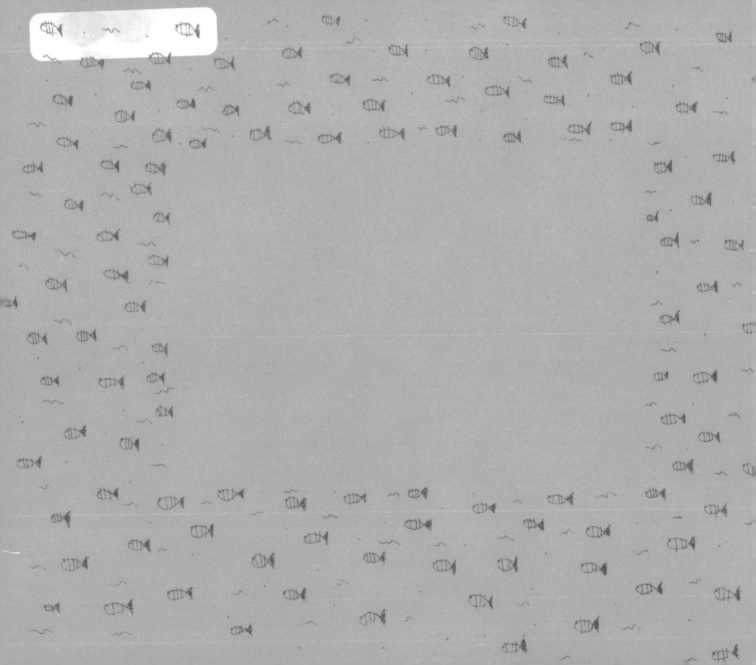

at the beach house

a guest book

sandy gingras

DOWN THE SHORE
PUBLISHING

The words "Down The Shore" and the Down The Shore Publishing logo are a registered U.S. Trademark.

Down The Shore Publishing Corp.
Box 100, West Creek, NJ 08092

www.down-the-shore.com

Printed in China
10 9 8

ISBN 1-59322-006-5

A guest book is a story told by many people. It's full of weather and salt and breezes. It's full of family and friends and strangers. It's full of what the tide was and when the sun shone. It's who ate over... It's what we ate. It's little things mostly, daily things. But it adds up to a life. You'd be surprised how it does. And what is ordinary today becomes a treasure over time.

We hope that this book is more than a record of who came to visit. We hope it's a journal of thoughts and stories, a scrapbook of memories. We left empty places for photos or doodles, a pocket for a ticket stub or a feather... there's room for thankfulness too.

name(s):

date of visit:

The weather was:

Some wonderful things we did:

what we saw & discovered:

moments & glimpses & little details that mattered:

Some other thoughts...

name(s):

date of visit:

The weather was:

Some wonderful things we did:

name(s):

date of visit:

The weather was:

Some wonderful things we did:

name(s):

date of visit:

The weather was:

Some wonderful things we did:

what we saw & discovered:

moments & glimpses & little details that mattered:

some other thoughts...

name(s):

date of visit:

The weather was:

Some wonderful things we did:

name(s):

date of visit:

The weather was:

Some wonderful things we did:

name(s):

date of visit:

The weather was:

Some wonderful things we did:

what we saw & discovered:

moments & glimpses & little details that mattered:

Some other thoughts...

name(s):

date of visit:

The weather was:

Some wonderful things we did:

name(s):

date of visit:

The weather was:

Some wonderful things we did:

name(s):

date of visit:

The weather was:

Some wonderful things we did:

what we saw & discovered:

moments & glimpses & little details that mattered:

Some other thoughts...

name(s):

date of visit:

The weather was:

Some wonderful things we did:

name(s):

date of visit:

The weather was:

Some wonderful things we did:

name(s):

date of visit:

The weather was:

Some wonderful things we did:

what we saw & discovered:

moments & glimpses & little details that mattered:

some other thoughts...

name(s):

date of visit:

The weather was:

Some wonderful things we did:

name(s):

date of visit:

The weather was:

Some wonderful things we did:

name(s):

date of visit:

The weather was:

Some wonderful things we did:

what we saw & discovered:

moments & glimpses & little details that mattered:

Some other thoughts...

name(s):

date of visit:

The weather was:

Some wonderful things we did:

---

name(s):

date of visit:

The weather was:

Some wonderful things we did:

name(s):

date of visit:

The weather was:

Some wonderful things we did:

what we saw & discovered:

moments & glimpses & little details that mattered:

Some other thoughts...

name(s):

date of visit:

The weather was:

Some wonderful things we did:

---

name(s):

date of visit:

The weather was:

Some wonderful things we did:

name(s):

date of visit:

The weather was:

some wonderful things we did:

what we saw & discovered:

moments & glimpses & little details that mattered:

some other thoughts...

name(s):

date of visit:

The weather was:

Some wonderful things we did:

name(s):

date of visit:

The weather was:

Some wonderful things we did:

name(s):

date of visit:

The weather was:

Some wonderful things we did:

what we saw & discovered:

moments & glimpses & little details that mattered:

Some other thoughts...

name(s):

date of visit:

The weather was:

some wonderful things we did:

name(s):

date of visit:

The weather was:

some wonderful things we did:

name(s):

date of visit:

The weather was:

Some wonderful things we did:

what we saw & discovered:

moments & glimpses & little details that mattered:

Some other thoughts...

name(s):

date of visit:

The weather was:

Some wonderful things we did:

name(s):

date of visit:

The weather was:

Some wonderful things we did:

name(s):

date of visit:

The weather was:

Some wonderful things we did:

what we saw & discovered:

moments & glimpses & little details that mattered:

Some other thoughts...

name(s):

date of visit:

The weather was:

Some wonderful things we did:

name(s):

date of visit:

The weather was:

Some wonderful things we did:

name(s):

date of visit:

The weather was:

some wonderful things we did:

what we saw & discovered:

moments & glimpses & little details that mattered:

some other thoughts...

name(s):

date of visit:

The weather was:

Some wonderful things we did:

name(s):

date of visit:

The weather was:

Some wonderful things we did:

name(s):

date of visit:

The weather was:

some wonderful things we did:

what we saw & discovered:

moments & glimpses & little details that mattered:

some other thoughts...

name(s):

date of visit:

The weather was:

Some wonderful things we did:

name(s):

date of visit:

The weather was:

Some wonderful things we did:

name(s):

date of visit:

The weather was:

Some wonderful things we did:

what we saw & discovered:

moments & glimpses & little details that mattered:

some other thoughts...

name(s):

date of visit:

The weather was:

Some wonderful things we did:

name(s):

date of visit:

The weather was:

Some wonderful things we did:

name(s):

date of visit:

The weather was:

Some wonderful things we did:

what we saw & discovered:

moments & glimpses & little details that mattered:

some other thoughts...

name(s):

date of visit:

The weather was:

Some wonderful things we did:

name(s):

date of visit:

The weather was:

Some wonderful things we did:

name(s):

date of visit:

The weather was:

Some wonderful things we did:

what we saw & discovered:

moments & glimpses & little details that mattered:

some other thoughts...

name(s):

date of visit:

The weather was:

some wonderful things we did:

---

name(s):

date of visit:

The weather was:

some wonderful things we did:

name(s):

date of visit:

The weather was:

Some wonderful things we did:

what we saw & discovered:

moments & glimpses & little details that mattered:

some other thoughts...

name(s):

date of visit:

The weather was:

Some wonderful things we did:

name(s):

date of visit:

The weather was:

Some wonderful things we did:

name(s):

date of visit:

The weather was:

Some wonderful things we did:

what we saw & discovered:

moments & glimpses & little details that mattered:

some other thoughts...

name(s):

date of visit:

The weather was:

Some wonderful things we did:

name(s):

date of visit:

The weather was:

Some wonderful things we did:

name(s):

date of visit:

The weather was:

Some wonderful things we did:

what we saw & discovered:

moments & glimpses & little details that mattered:

some other thoughts...

name(s):

date of visit:

The weather was:

Some wonderful things we did:

---

name(s):

date of visit:

The weather was:

Some wonderful things we did:

name(s):

date of visit:

The weather was:

Some wonderful things we did:

what we saw & discovered:

moments & glimpses & little details that mattered:

Some other thoughts...

name(s):

date of visit:

The weather was:

Some wonderful things we did:

name(s):

date of visit:

The weather was:

Some wonderful things we did:

name(s):

date of visit:

The weather was:

Some wonderful things we did:

what we saw & discovered:

moments & glimpses & little details that mattered:

Some other thoughts...

name(s):

date of visit:

The weather was:

Some wonderful things we did:

name(s):

date of visit:

The weather was:

Some wonderful things we did:

name(s):

date of visit:

The weather was:

Some wonderful things we did:

what we saw & discovered:

moments & glimpses & little details that mattered:

Some other thoughts...

name(s):

date of visit:

The weather was:

Some wonderful things we did:

name(s):

date of visit:

The weather was:

Some wonderful things we did:

name(s):

date of visit:

The weather was:

some wonderful things we did:

what we saw & discovered:

moments & glimpses & little details that mattered:

some other thoughts...

name(s):

date of visit:

The weather was:

Some wonderful things we did:

name(s):

date of visit:

The weather was:

Some wonderful things we did:

name(s):

date of visit:

The weather was:

Some wonderful things we did:

what we saw & discovered:

moments & glimpses & little details that mattered:

some other thoughts...

name(s):

date of visit:

The weather was:

some wonderful things we did:

name(s):

date of visit:

The weather was:

some wonderful things we did:

name(s):

date of visit:

The weather was:

Some wonderful things we did:

what we saw & discovered:

moments & glimpses & little details that mattered:

Some other thoughts...

name(s):

date of visit:

The weather was:

Some wonderful things we did:

name(s):

date of visit:

The weather was:

Some wonderful things we did:

name(s):

date of visit:

The weather was:

Some wonderful things we did:

what we saw & discovered:

moments & glimpses & little details that mattered:

Some other thoughts...

name(s):

date of visit:

The weather was:

Some wonderful things we did:

name(s):

date of visit:

The weather was:

Some wonderful things we did:

name(s):

date of visit:

The weather was:

Some wonderful things we did:

what we saw & discovered:

moments & glimpses & little details that mattered:

some other thoughts...

name(s):

date of visit:

The weather was:

Some wonderful things we did:

---

name(s):

date of visit:

The weather was:

Some wonderful things we did:

name(s):

date of visit:

The weather was:

Some wonderful things we did:

what we saw & discovered:

moments & glimpses & little details that mattered:

some other thoughts...